Praise

"These poems pull at the delic[...] versions of the truth desperatel[...] objects—provide the looking glass. Under Hahn's masterful hand, these *Foreign Bodies* feel quite familiar." —Stephanie Pruitt-Gaines, *BookPage*

"The fact that such an intellectually diverse, formally dexterous, deeply personal, stylistically rich, and brazenly experimental [collection] could cohere into a solid whole, that she could assemble work from such disparate aspects of life, from such varied interests and emotional origins, and form a sturdy amalgamation that is so unified that it seems that if even one poem were removed it wouldn't be complete—shows just how brilliant and singular a poet Hahn is."

—Jonathan Russell Clark, *Vol. 1 Brooklyn*

"Under [Hahn's] exquisite vision . . . familiar objects assume the feel of the sacred. . . . [H]er precise physical descriptions and scientific observations are juxtaposed against the writing's exuberance."

—*Publishers Weekly*, starred review

"Kimiko Hahn writes with a particular brightness of mind like no one else—or maybe with just enough kinship to Marianne Moore and their shared weirdness to mention it here, their glorious fascination with the particular-peculiars of nature and human behavior. . . . Where another poet, doing such inexhaustible research, would eventually clean up her act, Kimiko Hahn in *Foreign Bodies* makes as much art out of documentary evidence and 'sparkly' research as she does elegance, memory, or lyrical compression." —David Baker, author of *Swift*

"'Notice that the simplest often yields the most,' writes Kimiko Hahn in her tenth collection, wherein the smallest of relics become powerful portals through time, space, and memory. With expert lyric sensibility and all the anguish of daughterhood, *Foreign Bodies* reminds us of the necessity of poetry as a spell for intimacy. It's a spell that offers hope of the most urgent kind: the hope of closing the gap between 'my other's body' and 'my mother's body,' between ourselves and all that we can't reach."

—Franny Choi, author of *Soft Science*

"Kimiko Hahn's structurally and formally complex new book, *Foreign Bodies*, is a long, rich meditation on detail. It is a masterpiece of scale. Just as the cellular biologist works backward from a single cell under an electron microscope to the full organism, so Hahn works from the minute, ephemeral stuff left from a life (a loose thread, a single hair, an open safety pin) back to the overarching themes of memory, death, love, and sorrow. The book is a series of elegies of the most original and surprising sort. A quite miraculous performance."   —Lynn Emanuel, author of *The Nerve of It*

FOREIGN
BODIES

FOREIGN BODIES

POEMS

KIMIKO HAHN

W. W. NORTON & COMPANY
Independent Publishers Since 1923

For information about permission to reproduce selections from this book, write to
Permissions, W. W. Norton & Company, Inc., 500 Fifth Avenue, New York, NY 10110

For information about special discounts for bulk purchases, please contact
W. W. Norton Special Sales at specialsales@wwnorton.com or 800-233-4830

Manufacturing by LSC Communications, Harrisonburg
Book design by JAM Design
Production manager: Beth Steidle

Library of Congress Cataloging-in-Publication Data

Names: Hahn, Kimiko, 1955– author.
Title: Foreign bodies : poems / Kimiko Hahn.
Description: First Edition. | New York, NY : W. W. Norton & Company, [2020] |
Includes bibliographical references.
Identifiers: LCCN 2019045939 | ISBN 9781324005216 (hardcover) |
ISBN 9781324005223 (epub)
Subjects: LCGFT: Poetry.
Classification: LCC PS3558.A32357 F67 2020 | DDC 811/.54—dc23
LC record available at https://lccn.loc.gov/2019045939

ISBN 978-0-393-88244-5 pbk.

W. W. Norton & Company, Inc., 500 Fifth Avenue, New York, N.Y. 10110
www.wwnorton.com

W. W. Norton & Company Ltd., 15 Carlisle Street, London W1D 3BS

1 2 3 4 5 6 7 8 9 0

Some things move in and dig down

                                    whether you want them to or not.

   Like pieces of small glass your body subsumes when you are young . . .

                                           —CHARLES WRIGHT

Contents

FOREIGN
BODIES

Unearthly Delights

After you rip through the screen
and wedge yourself into Father's bedroom,
you find a pile of art supply catalogs,
brown scraps of bedspread,
cotton batting, a rodent body, rodent turds,
and tiny white naked human creatures
flipped topsy-turvy to skewer
down the ass and out the mouth
in the primordial ooze that is manifestly
the brimstone and bile of this book left open
to Bosch's realm beneath the left hand of God,
my foxed legacy of human bonfire.

·   ·   ·

Object Lessons

From Chevalier Quixote Jackson

> What might happen to the collection if we let narrative
> and desire back in?
>
> MARY CAPPELLO

To answer a wish to possess:
tuck a chess piece into a cheek.
To meet a hunger not to share:
swallow a kewpie doll whole.
To recall the rubber of a nipple:
suck on a pencil eraser.
Safe-keep sincere assemblage

by stowing in a ribcage. Yes,
                            now I lay my
two pressed pennies
down to constant tissue.

·

Like Dr. Chevalier Quixote Jackson,
nineteenth-century laryngologist who

removed from tiny upper bodies
an involved collection of objects

—nails and bolts, radiator key,
a child's perfect attendance pin,

a Carry-Me-For-Luck medallion—

to lay into trays of cotton, yes,
like him, each child had hoarded some thing

in her inmost chest.

•

Yes, because children crawl on the treacherous floor,
Chevalier, if I may,
                 removed then preserved every last one
along with stunning x-rays of needles

lodged in a small patient's lung. Also
a charm in the shape of a hound. Perhaps

the hound who rescued him in childhood.
Perhaps a jar of charms that won't leave go one's origin.

(Perhaps *my* pooch who calms my errant heartbeats down.)

·

Origins: crime or act of preservation:
Saturn devoured his children

to save his own skin from divine betrayal.
Snow White's stepmother devoured

the girl's lung and liver—or so she believed.

My youngest, after Mother died, figured,
Grandma now lives inside my tummy

with dog and bird and fishy.

·

According to one biographer: *at one point other children blindfolded Jackson*
and threw him into a coal pit, and he was rescued only after some mutt happened
to find him unconscious.

·

In my cigar box, a swallow

                              nest of pine

lined with feathers, bits of birch bark, and trash

for comfort can coincide with comforting;

from the shred of blankie inside her purse to

his rabbit-foot keychain

to the hair she plucks and swallows

in a cycle of self-harm called *Rapunzel*.

Chevalier archived them in shallow drawers

according to their kind.

The two girls could not unlock the door to their father's home. The girls could not open a window for the medical books leaning against the panes. The girls could neither pry open the bathroom window painted shut nor the cellar door where the carton of bleach and cans of stew were stacked against it. They could not find a ladder to climb to the bedroom window and check on a mahogany bedroom set—this, they knew to be surrounded by trash bags of mother's clothing that they'd tagged years ago for the Salvation Army. And, hopefully, on the nightstand, there was still a collection of ivory netsuke.

Also, a reclining ivory nude, female, used by nineteenth-century doctors.

The girls wondered what he made of that woman.

The doctor's x-rays captured
miniature binoculars, silver horse-charm, four open safety pins

lodged between tiny ribs.
Each feels like a story's climax

when the heroine, dropping into a cave,
discovers a treasure at bottom

that cannot be removed unless she answers these three questions:

What is the opposite of "cleave"?
Who savors rampion?
Why not rock an empty chair?

How to extract an open safety pin without scarring?
How to save the object without anesthesia?
How to preserve all two thousand foreign bodies?

•

A child crawls on the treacherous floor
appraising every object inside her mouth.

•

Dr. Jackson produced the modern endoscope with the use of hollow tubes
and illumination. To see inside. As if he could see the image of the horse-
beating that had taken residence inside him like a *primal scene,* told him
where his body began and ended . . .

In the Emergency Room, surgeons also remove sex-related objects
        from the rectum (the ubiquitous light bulb or hamster)

                and from the perineum (straight pins and nails)
                    and from the penis (rose stem with thorns).

    There's also the stripper flashing a razor in and out of her labia.

                        Alas, my imagination pales—

                        •

Newly coined terms—
Amylophagia, ingesting laundry starch
Cautopyreiophagia, ingesting burnt matches
Geomelophagia, raw potatoes
—all exemplifying specialized terms

within *Pica,* a disorder named after the Eurasian magpie *pica pica,*
known for its *morbid craving.*

(What does one turn to
when laundry starch, say, becomes no more—?)

Flashlight, trombone cleaner,
curling iron, screw, battery: all up the bum!

•

In the local Savings & Trust I descend to the corridor below street level.
A woman sits in a cool gray light updating client info, filing her nails,
text messaging. I step up to the bulletproof window, slip my ID into
the slot, smile, and wait. She looks from my photo to my face. "Which
one?" she asks. "The smaller one," I reply. I am not able to say my ex-
husband's name in this ceremony of twenty years. "Yes," she replies.
And as she takes her key and mine, I think about this box as *incomplete
transaction*: old wedding bands, diamond earrings twice worn, and
Mother's jewelry—inherited and rarely worn. No—never worn. Safe keep.
Kept here. From myself.

Then there are bonds for the children. (I haven't ever checked the other
one containing the deed with the new husband.)

What is down the hatch?
(A penny-sized harmonica, a pea-sized magnet, button batteries, jacks!)

What then is the fourth question?
(*What does that mean*, safe?)

To whom does the extracted foreign body belong?
(If you tuck a crucifix under your tongue, Mama then can't hunt it down.)

Too hard to swallow? Or, swallow hard?
(Nicole's missing charms: sewing machine, thimble, *Mother*)

The why:
playing around wicker chair
playing with a tin cup containing a white pearl button
alone on floor with lucky-shell bracelet
put toy in his mouth to hide from sister
child alone in room found hairpin under pillow
bored or unhappy

•

Dr. Jackson's Aphorisms:
Let your left hand know what your right hand does and how to do it.
Let your mistakes worry you enough to prevent repetition.
Nature helps, but she is no more interested in the survival of your patient
    than in the survival of the attacking pathogenic bacteria.

•

Yes, how to extract a barrette without further scarring?
How to store the object of your ardor, even to stay what harms
(junk drawer, purse, . . . flash drive)?

Yes, how to *persevere*
long enough to sound an alarm? to be alarming?

Somewhere I have a palm-sized clock,
green with a cartoon face,
that Daddy bought for me at the hospital
when we visited Mother, who'd just had a baby.
And could that toy

be tucked away with puka-shells, miniature sleigh, and
—and really, has the point of *an object lesson* come down to this—
Mother's plastic collar *stay*?

A Dusting

However Mother has reappeared
—say, as motes on a feather duster—
scientists say the galaxy
was thus created. This daybreak
she seeds a cumulous cloud.

·

Wherever Mother is bound
she's joined *ashes ashes*
or dirt underfoot or bits
off Tower North and Tower South.
Repurpose does not arrive whole cloth.

From stardust, dust bunnies,
Dust Bowl and *Dust unto Dust*

to Ruykeyser's *silica*, Whitman's *boot-soles*
and Dunbar's *What of his love, what of his lust?*

to the samples that astronomers collect—
dust is where the sparrow bathes herself.

"Not a cloud in the sky,"
Mother says as she hangs the laundry outside,
Father paints *en plein air,*
and we girls sweep crumbs under the rug.
This summer, Father sees
Inferno everywhere.

•

No dustups from little girls!
As a consequence, one scribbled
on the dust-bins of history
and the other dusted
for fingerprints. And the mother?
The mother lived in a vacuum.

•

Inside the senseless corridors
the daughter cannot respire.
Inside the vulgar cosmic
the mother cannot be revived
in streaming wet traffic.

Nowadays, I lie down in the sunlight
to see my mama
moting around as sympathetic ash.
Yes, one morning whether misty or yellow
I'll be soot with her—

elegiac and original.

The Old House Speaks

Before I became foundation, I was a chicken-coop aways from farmhouse, carriage house and barn. And around my grounds, someone's daughter played with her bisque baby. Among stink and chicken feathers. Eggshells. Nests.

I tasted the haze of dandruff and chicken shit. The taste of my own throat.

From my planks and wire I heard the clucks. The coos. The tap-tap tap-tap as the scabby rooster pecked like the son's paddle-toy.

I wasn't so much humble as meager. There is nowhere for anywhere except a runaway who kneads the dank, brown, soiled straw.

The farmer's little girl played with chipped teacups alongside the buzzing kitchen scraps. All converted, finally, into a trash heap.

·

Noisy and noisome. From that rough roost to an indoor-out: branch and ice rip me open. Birds tear into my screens, leave droppings all over my insides.

Did I say *a runaway*? More recently, down the hill in one family's garage, the wife turned the car on and fell asleep to the smell of gas—shutting the door to other neighbor's rat-a-tat-tat.

The male raccoon leaves shitty paw prints on the grocery circulars and coupons that flood the floorboards. Even on watercolors left out on a desk. There is nowhere where there is no scat.

After winter torpor, I wince when the raccoon births her kits in a closet.

Some say a raccoon makes over two hundred sounds—and it's true, I've counted as many.

And the mask, reduces glare at night.

And the ringed tail, stores fat for the winter and aids in any balancing act.

And the dousing of food, yes, "wash."

Funny how the pregnant female kicks out the male.

Yes, where creatures thrive, I cannot breathe—

What will become of my kitchen? The room where the now-middle-aged woman, when a toddler, sat in the bright porcelain sink for a sponge bath. One of the few events that she cares to recall while sifting through the rubbish, once her mother's home, her father's house. Or was it the inverse?

charms i.

Mindful

Collect a sand dollar from dry sand
And not from silted shallows
While wet it's very much alive
And will consign its sorrows

. . .

Constant Objection

More often than not, a house fills up
with only stifled objections
to a dozen glue guns, a case of Brillo pads,
jars of preserves. But—coffee cans
of chewed up chewing gum
is why he resided alone.

•

Notice that the simplest often yields the most:
OBJECT: *body, doodad, meaning, purpose,*
hope, butt, . . . to mind and *to resist.*
The theory itself yields: Pinky-Bear,
Blankie, Sock-Puppet, Nightmare.

•

Objection? Outside a neighboring clinic
three fundamentalists wait
to shoot the doctor at point-blank range.
Meantime, Father saw Medusa
on the clothes line, under the sink,
in a tureen of string beans.

He drew the mythic ball of live hair
that no one can stand or he'll turn to stone.
Then there's cherry-red on her toes.
Then there's his own weekend Father
taking him to see "Boxing Kangaroos"
who turned out to be yawning strippers.

On objectification, Marx wrote:
As values, all commodities are only
definite masses of congealed labour time.
Yes, Hamburger Helper, trombone, robot vacuum!

Yes, covert kiwi or flagrant heroin!

(As for the coffee can of chewed up chewing gum—
just a necrophile's faithful rite
to resuscitate a strict mama,
viewed on the Discovery Channel.)

•

After tossing her clothes and cosmetics
I crisscrossed the city on a bus:
peering out at the concrete,
cherry blossoms fell in my hair
from no open window. They piped up,
How much more can a daughter object?

Before I swept every speck of you

from the rooms where Father would carry on—

if only I'd saved your brush

with a few strands of silver hair.

Mother, dear object of my despondence,
What more can a daughter bear?

A Little Safe

In a toy safe, I locked
seven glass giraffes from Grandma
once displayed on her credenza.
After she lost her riddled lung,

the hospital lost all her remains.
Or so the story goes.

•

I treasure her charm,
a tiny box housing a dollar—
not that that would get me far in a pinch.
And, speaking of pinches, she said:

Don't let a boy into your purse.
But, what does a mother rehearse?

•

On Wednesdays, half the fifth grade
left for Catechism Class, each

to learn to save my soul
as if the chest, a cathedral. When

a cousin stepped out on his wife,
I called his other woman *a buttress*
and added, *You'd best send her flying.*

•

What I locked in my school locker
besides pop quizzes marked *C*,
a velvet coat, and *Tiger Beats*:

a locket. From no one.
Like evidence in a cold case file
of thirteen hacked-up call girls.

If I could visit Antarctica
I'd visit a penguin papa on his long-winded stint
warming an egg on his feet. Still,

a girl should not show her *pieds* ever
when around her father.

Yes, even in unkind terrain
the girl felt okay on a trek with a coyote

until they reached the apathetic border
and her heart broke off
its eight years of beating. The same
for the boy in the trunk. For

the hundreds of babies in tents.
I find the stories are the faithful ones.

After Grandma lost her riddled lung,
the raccoon ransacked emergency
boxes of powdered milk in the pantry.

Cold cases of Squirt remained safe.
And the word, *safety*? Think rubbers. Think patrol.
Think *Glock*. Then think accidental discharge.

I found that in the Isua supracrustal belt,

flora was frozen for billions of years,
secure until discovery. Throughout his home
Father entrusted his critical papers

to those catacombs of no recollection.

Hatchlings

Though tough to experiment
on a crocodile in the wild,
laboratory research has yielded
that prior to hatching,
a little one begins to coo.
Why?
To signal to the mama,
start digging?
To cue siblings to coo
for a synchronous emergence?
Or to practice wheedling
for pastime or coddle? Or
perhaps to rehearse the menace
that even a crocodile must acquire?
Maybe, though, cooing is fun. How
to research what transpires
in the head of a hatchling
before it's hatched—
and why we need to know—
might well be an intimacy
not meant to be trespassed.

•   •   •

The Ashes

The puppy snarfles to be let out
and I wake to radiator gurgling
then feet crunching the reticent snow.
Before I was born, Mother sewed her own suits.
What do her ashes know?

Father shoved snow off the supine roof.
Mother crafted Christmas ornaments:
glue and glitter and red balls.
No tinsel, no angels.
Her death started in the living room.

For bonsai, pliers the size of a nail clipper,
spools of wire, and a fist-sized rock.
One bore a petite pomegranate,
never to eat, not to touch.
Her death began with a baseball bat.

In the vineyard, he secured the strongest cane
from training stake to fruiting wire.
Pruning with handsaw and lopper.
He'd leave a spur for the next season.
He shoved her away with direct objects.

•

In a cold snap if one pipe freezes,
the rest may freeze as well.
Even before the puppy stirs.
Even before a baby sister arrived
in Mother's arms in the misleading car.

•

After the war, after she met Father,
she smoked menthols but didn't cha-cha anymore.
She'd light up and blow smoke
out the apoplectic window.
He found the ashes on the sill.

Fireflies winked for mates or prey
outside the savvy window of my own first home
where I sewed a dress too smart to wear.
On the stereo, a bluesman cried,
I need my ashes hauled!

I tucked away our baby's pink layette
in circumspect mothballs
for a christening that never took place.
As well, a doll that Auntie crocheted.
More than anything, I love tidal pools.

·

I know her ashes are at Father's,
lost in his charnel of junk mail.
He claims that thieves have stolen the box,
his knob cutter and root hook.
He says, *ashes aren't remains anyways*.

·

Winter stripped everything to limb
and dejected nest. No angels, no crèche.
I don't know whose recollections are suspect:
after leaving Maui, Mother learned to swim.
(She loved tidal pools more than anything.)

·

In my kitchen, logs blink in the fire—
through blinds, the wind blusters and
browbeaten trees creak in the orchard.
The rain pours then stops for sun. If
he lost Mother's ashes what more could I stand?

Omusubi tastes best on black beaches.
Because Mother never learned to swim,
she watched her five brothers from a blanket.
On the intransigent subway, I can't recall if I've passed
my station. Metal smells of being fertile again.
(His mother said *her social station—*)

Mother showed our little girl how to sift flour
and how to crank an egg beater.
After Father lost her,
he barred us from his rooms and from his yard
where at night, long red worms
slithered up from the ground.

Mother's ashes know: before the puppy snarfles,
Father shoves snow off the supine roof;
for bonsai, use pliers the size of a nail clipper;
in the vineyard, the strongest canes;
in a cold snap, a hair dryer on frozen pipes;
fireflies winked for mates or prey outside
while I tucked away my baby's pink layette.
Mother's ashes know their box is in the living room
where she didn't cha-cha anymore.
Where has winter stripped everything to the nest?
In my kitchen, the logs blink in the fire and I know
omusubi tastes best on a *back* shore. I know, too,
she doggedly showed granddaughters how to graft flowers.

charms ii.

Sympathy

When you spy a horseshoe crab
Flipped over on the shore
Right it gently in the tide
And with your kin—a true rapport

•   •   •

Sparkly Things

Ephemera, mouse droppings,
pillows torn to feathers:

Father stays to nest
while the magpie knows in its bones
a hollow for flight

and a collarbone fused for stability.
Her collarbone had shown off

pearls, lapis lazuli, the coral from Tibet.
The strands are buried here,
my mother, long gone. Here, too,

I flew down the stairs when I was a child.
He slipped a few steps
covered in ice and leaves. He hit his head.

He is not a bird.

·

Its collarbone was confused
with the one for wishes. I wish
he had not lost Mother

·

to that house where the calico
ate one of her own.
Do magpies commit such things?
Yes, and flip over dung
in search of beetles conjugating there,
a secret hoard kept in a cupboard. Funny—
now we know these crow-cousins
actually fear
                    sparkly things.

My two cousins flew to Mother's funeral,
fogged with incense—

not as august as a magpie who discovers its dead
and summons the others to raucously convene

before flying off, done with their patter.
Also not like a magpie,
he doesn't recognize himself in a mirror.

The Cryptic Chamber

For authorities whose hopes
are shaped by mercenaries?

MARIANNE MOORE

The nautilus, altering little from its Cambrian form,
jubilantly paddles about
by drawing water with a siphon
in and out of her living chamber;

then jet-propelling, adjusting buoyancy, and diffusing salt,
she whirls along sand and rock. Unknowingly

my beloved gave me such a shell—
an endangered thing
as well as a house that holds a mother.

                            •

I love that this mollusk,
coupling, spawning just once a year,

and whose eggs take nearly as long to hatch—I
love that ancient Greeks named her *nautilus*

ναυτίλος 'sailor'

believing she—or he—used two expanded arms as sails.
In my mind, crucifix or a child's snow angel.

Since the opalescent inner shell

passes as pearl,
escalating its own slaughter,

my cabinet is no longer curious:

now, I'm satisfied with a hornet's nest from the backyard,

snake skin found on a footpath,
coil of whelk cases from the local beach,

and, also from the beach, a stone in the shape of Jizo,

so like the statue we saw in Shibuya,
bobby pins clipped to its red bib.

                                        a   complex

"lustrous coil"

                    erects

                        buoyancy

Those logarithmic spirals, naturalists suggest,
echo the arms of hurricanes and distant galaxies,

taking fifteen years to mature, fixing
the prized creature to a marine list

of those soon eradicated or
left to natural history diorama,

art exhibit, jewelry box. I've already
spoken of my mother's coral necklace,

inherited then stowed away
in my safe deposit box, away even from memory

until I turned in the key and there it was:

a whorl of sharp red beads
that fastened with what my father called *sister-hooks.*

(To the list of things soon to vanish
add coral *and* the Hawai'ian language?)

                a relatively large brain
                          like the hull of a submarine
can   serve as a

parrot

                                    •

                a relatively large   eye   can

        implode—like

home

After all, I believe Design is *design*.
Still, I can also believe that the *order of the universe*

—including the one in my hands,
a shell cast in calcium and, when swimming about,

whose eyes peer through tentacles—
is mathematically mysterious. But

I'm not so romantic that I can't see
extinct as natural—

I know that but she's lasted so long—
                                        a living fossil
safe if it weren't for designated squalor—

                              •

a dollar a shell to thwart misery, I get—

                        with baited   depth

the
                Landman

        stunned   perfect spirals

Cryptic

When seen from above, the shell is darker in color
and marked with irregular stripes,
which helps it blend into the dark water below.
The underside, almost completely white,
makes the animal indistinguishable
from the brighter waters near the surface.

This shell colouration keeps the animal cryptic.

cups and pitchers

begin a formal

horror show

 •

                                      the curved

arms of   Florence   turned
                    gold and rubies

                            into danger

●

I know I know—a dollar isn't merely pedestrian.
I know that some sell the chambered nautilus for their living.

I know I'm guilty of such purchase
and do nothing to give away or give way

to the distraught
so soon there'll be nothing left—

but I know that no Designer would have such eradication in mind.

I know, too, that collectors have a passion for panic—

·

Curiosities
A floating poem after Adrienne

A plastic wishbone

A pearl button inside a plastic baby mug

Strands of black and gray hair tied with embroidery thread—
Mother's?—I don't recall—

Dad's jackknife with mother-of-pearl handle (From his father? Did his
father give him any thing?)

Plastic scrimshaw pendant of a whale, a souvenir from Lahaina before
my sister was born

Harold's scrimshawed whale tooth

A wishbone

A doll's guide to *Kiyoto* lodged inside a walnut, a bracelet from an
elephant's single hair, a *Royal Hawaiian* matchbox of sand, a plastic
compass taken from sister

Kabuki ticket stubs

Mother's choker of spiked coral beads from Florence that I now possess

·

envoy

below the range of   *sunlight*

                    the larger order of the universe
    chambers

            alarms

        ·   ·   ·

Notes on March 10, 1992

Returning home on that March night, Father stopped at a traffic light, then turned left toward the parkway ramp. An oncoming car ran the red and broadsided them.

According to the detective: around 11 pm in a nearby parking lot, a group of boys, white and armed with baseball bats, threatened two Pakistani youth. The altercation whipped into a car chase, the two ran a red light and hit Father's car. The white kids slowed to look, then sped off.

Mother had said, "I'm going to rest my eyes." Father must have told me—but who knows since he doesn't even recall the stoplight.

The detective informed me, "Your mother died instantly." That EMS had attempted to resuscitate her on the road. It was raining.

He also informed me that Father was at Yonkers General. My sister and I drove up to find him in the ER. He asked after Mother. When we told him she was dead, he shouted *No No No*. Before we left him to nod off, he asked us to notify a colleague.

Two days later, she was at the hospital with a homemade cake.

Now, clearing out his house these decades later, I am surprised to find the ticket stubs, either saved or forgotten. I do know that somewhere in the drifts of debris there is a skull that Father had used as a sketching model. All during our childhood he kept it in a coat closet, but in recent years took it out to pass along to a painter friend. Eventually, he forgot the skull's whereabouts but noted to the friend, "Probably still in its plastic shopping bag."

Holding the Kabuki tickets in my hand, I ask myself why Father—with all the rubbish he has told us—has never wondered out loud if before turning, he could have looked one more second to see the car careening toward them.

Last week, Father did say that he and his brother were out of touch. I said, "Uncle died decades ago. When he was 27." I did not remind him that his brother had shot himself. Nor did I tell him that I believed the skull was taking revenge—against Uncle having smuggled it back from the war, and against Father for accepting it.

I am not looking for the skull, but know I might stumble across it.

I know I would have believed that I'd killed her.

· · ·

Another Poem for Maude

What would her lips feel *like*—? A tulip petal? A porcelain bowl?

The last time I saw her she was waving goodbye as Ted and I drove off with the baby, already snoozing in the backseat. I saw her turn away to climb the three dozen steps back to the shambly house. Not her fault, the shambles. Not the fault of mice or the snow that settled into a crust on the flat roof.

Days later, Father took her to the theater. On the drive home, a car of teenagers broadsided them. Father cursed. Mother lay slumped on the passenger side. He didn't realize she was dead.

A metal bowl? Doily? Birch bark? Page torn from an old book?

Ted and I decided to see her at the funeral home. To "view her" in the pine coffin. Before she was delivered to the crematorium. The undertaker commented on how "Orientals don't show their age." Sixty-eight, only a few years older than I am today. I looked. But I didn't clip a wisp of hair as keepsake. I didn't touch her clothes or her hand. It was enough to see what I would come to describe as *the body that was Mother's.*

Ice? Mother once told me not to put lips or tongue on ice because the delicate skin would stick fast.

Was I afraid to kiss her on the lips, the lips that were my mother's? Did sense even occur to me? Pumice? Bar of soap? *Like* both fastens and keeps at arm's length.

(Had she wanted to go?)

.   .   .

charms iii.

Trustfulness

Never take from a father's shelf
Impressions of ancient reptile
Or you'll fossilize your heart
And forever bleed out bile

.   .   .

She Sells Seashells

Considering the Life of Mary Anning

When high tide withdraws
a shell burrows down with its foot
and should that muck harden,
the razor, say, may petrify
over millennia:

such demise may be a little girl's good fortune.
Especially in 1811.

.

If only I believed in talismans
especially in regard to my dragonfly

possessed by stone for eons:
to make ends meet
Mary climbed a local cliff with tools
to pry out spirals—*snake stones*—

she'd sell to neighbors convinced
of their charming powers.

Mary was named
after her departed sister
who'd tossed sawdust on the kitchen hearth,
inspiring flames to her bib
and burning her to bits. Me,

I was instructed to so fear a match
when the lesson came to strike one
I twisted, shrieked, and wept. But

the penniless Annings scraped by
against the raw ocean air—

The *verteberries, sea lilies, scuttle* and *thunderstones*
had lodged in strata for millennia
above the English Channel and below
the Annings' dark dank cottage. By the Saw Mill River,

my own parents stratified seeds in their garden
though weeds disallowed them
to seek the light of day ever.

Miss *She-sells-seashells-on-the-seashore*,
after a furious storm, found a flying dragon
in the Lyme Regis sediment.
Often gone all day alone
turbulence was her best companion

revealing where to look for bones.
I found an egg dyed yellow and green.
I found my mother when she'd died—I mean,
when she'd *hide*.

I did not find an Ammon's horn.
I did find a piece of matzo beneath a tablecloth.
And I found my mother dead to which

a cousin asked, "What does that mean,
'to *find* someone dead'? Lackluster? Uncaring?
Without a mirror for her little girl?"

Bleeding-tooth and *pelican foot,*
Venus comb murex, keyhole limpet—

a hobby for some, for the Annings
bought bread, maybe mutton, maybe
The Dissenters' Theological Magazine.

Still, I wish I could've chiseled out a Plesiosaurus—
especially to query Genesis—to discover
something as stupendous as extinction.

After a common storm Mr. Anning fell from a ledge,
suffering till he died. Mary's dog

similarly perished just feet from where she stood.
I wouldn't want to pry into stone
over the swirling coast that cost so much.
Mary didn't possess any such choice

and faced rude currents to stay afloat:

·

They say Miss Anning attends Col. Birch

These men of learning have sucked her brains

Richard "Dinosaur" Owen rarely stooped to dirty his hands in the field

Coprolite (fossilized feces) finely illustrated

Mary untangled seaweed from the dead woman's hair

·

To Darwin's professor she wrote, *[the find looks like] a skeleton with a head
like a pair of scissors . . . analogous to nothing.* Even so, the geologist paid no
attention to her *transitional creature.*

Mary's a very clever funny Creature
said Dr. Featherstonhaugh as he purchased
the spine of a sea beast she'd found. My aunt

said that shells can be alive.
Some are left-handed, some right. Most

have a door and a foot. *Very* funny, I thought,
determined next holiday to search low and high.

King Frederick visited the Anning's Fossil Depot
to purchase an ichthyosaur—
the crocodile with flippers, the undulating fish lizard—

was it Mary's torso? brother Joseph's skull?
or was the skeleton complete?
Strange how the body is so
undependable except at the last moment.

Some baby shells swim about,
others dig into mud flats
or latch onto random stone and stem.
When my own babies settled into silt

I had to rake them out

just as my mother'd coaxed with indulgences.
Mary's mother at first forbade her

to clamber up those cliffs
scolded by tide and sea mist, but,
in the end, feared more the ubiquitous poorhouse.

Some shells have eyes. All have mouth and anus
employed to move along. I've watched
a sand dollar drag its pattern in the silt,
a beautiful primal moment. In Mary's time,

marked by the reign of a Queen,
even a twenty-foot fossil gave a woman no purchase.

Some shells leap out of water!
Some leap off a boat's deck

back into a more kindred habitat!
Mary bought her own house
so she could properly dust and polish
the so-called curiosities that evolved into
patriarchal—I mean, *paleontological* import.

Not so odd that a soft fleshy creature
builds a stony home
—smooth, ribbed, warty, or spiny—

from a fold excreting particles of lime.
More strange is a creature of flesh
who can't protect herself thus

regardless of cranium or cul-de-sac residence.

•

In her commonplace book, Mary transcribed
'Tis time this heart should be unmoved,
            Since others it hath ceased to move . . .
and notes on physics and astronomy.
On large sheets of paper, she sketched the creatures
she could not present at London's Geological Society
in person. On my typewriter, I exhumed

all sorts of impressions whether
prehistoric or from my childhood bedroom.

•

Although the warty professors visited her seaside home,
bartered then took credit for her finds

when all was done and said again
she who sold seashells found fossils

more stellar than a tongue twister,

having had the *Black Ven* as taskmistress.

envoy:

she-sells-seashells-on-the-seashore

sold the so-called curios
some have eyes
some coprolite
most have a door and a foot

some baby shells swim about
below the coastal cliff near her home
near bleeding-tooth and pelican foot

and their healing powers but

no one wants to puzzle over
an overhanging house or stony abode or
a funny tongue-twister but

with or without a charm

a little girl can fashion a mirror of her own

•   •   •

Likeness

A Self-Portrait

Like Professor Sara Lewis   I view the meadow as theater
for *passion and yearning*   *courtship duets*
       competitions for affection
         cruel deception and gruesome death
Like the Professor   *fluent in firefly*   I am fluent in
    on-the-fly   and   on-the-sly
      when circumstances are   well   well lit

           •

Like a female firefly   I am *remarkably picky*
     when checking out flashy males
because *long-lasting pulses*
    mean a lot   when it comes to   say   *nuptial gifts*
     —packages of protein injected with sperm—

furthermore   it's crucial to pay attention
      yes I tell my daughters

           pay attention to attention

Unlike male fireflies
        who *do not need to burn many extra calories*
    to make flashes
            because only a *tiny* bit of energy is needed
I do
    burn a lot of fuel in the service of being flashy:
                shimmying at Danceteria
acting-out at the Nuyorican
    leafletting at Kentile
                    to overthrow The Man

And what can I say?
　　　　like the cannibal　　Photuris firefly that
　　pounces　　*bites*　　then　　*sucks the blood*

of the special other
　　　　　　　　for ill-tasting chemicals
which it utilizes for protection
　　　　well, me, too—

　　　　I take her in　　　　to ward her off

　　　　　　　　　　•

There is also trickery　　in the case　　of the Photuris firefly
who at times　　*sits on a blade of grass, responding*
　　to male fireflies with deceptive flashes

　　　　mimic　　deceive　　devour

like legend　　like fairy tale
　　　　　　like office copy-room

Regrettably   I've never sat in my backyard the night before
        heading off to Belize
                        unlike Professor Sara Lewis
who   found herself
                        —instead of mulling over coral reefs—
        espying firefly sexual selection and
comparing the winks to Darwin's thesis on
                        male displays of antlers and feathers

though it is true   that at the book launch where Harold read *Bestial*
        I took note   of his commanding backlist

Lastly   also like fireflies   what I cook up
        can present *an unpleasant meal*
although mine   does not glow
        although I wish I could produce glowy things
            —sestina, sukiyaki, manifesto—
      However, like firefly glow
I turned on during courtship   Harold said so and

        he   himself   is brilliant
                        especially at nightfall

—though not from enzymes in his tail—

· · ·

charms iv.

Nip in the Bud

Pull out a Queen Anne's Lace
By every gnarled tendril
To hone your skill at tatting
As well as thwart a rival

•

Reprisal

If a sweetheart aims to stray
For a neighbor's tryst
Find a way to shake a branch
Of nettles on her sheets

•   •   •

Foreign Body

This is a poem on my other's body,
I mean, *my mother's body*, I mean the one

who saved her braid of blue-black hair
in a drawer, I mean the one

I could lean against—
against as in insistence. Fuzzy-dress-of-wuzzy

one. Red-lipstick one.
Rubber-gloves one. Her one to me,

bad-ger bad-ger

or so I heard. The one body I write on—
her sun-flecked body

as she bathed in the afternoon.
Was I five? It was Summer.

Then Winter—where today
I call the unlocked bathroom to mind:

I cannot leave her body alone.

Which is how I found Mother
escaping the heat of a 1950s house,

Father on a ladder with blowtorch
to scrape the paint off the outside.

                                  •

badger badger

                                  •

The sun in those suburbs
simmered the tar roof over our rooms

in the town where the wasps lived
inside paper cells beneath both eaves and roots.

They sing—
      I mean—sting very much, the wasps.

                                  •

Now I'm sixty. Sweet as dried papaya.

My hair, a bit tarnished,
my inmost, null.

Memory is falling away
as if an image shattered to shards then

re-collected for a kaleidoscope:

I click the pieces into sharp arrangement—
bad bad girl girl
In turn, a daughter turns sovereign.

                    •   •   •

After Being Asked If I Write the *Occasional Poem*

After leaving Raxruhá, after
crossing Mexico with a coyote,
after reaching at midnight
that barren New Mexico border,
a man and his daughter
looked to Antelope Wells
for asylum and were arrested. After
forms read in Spanish
to the Mayan-speaking father,
after a cookie but no water, after
the wait for the lone bus
to return for their turn, after boarding,
after the little girl's temperature spiked,
she suffered two heart attacks,
vomited, and stopped breathing. After
medics revived the seven-year-old
at Lordsburg Station, after
she was flown to El Paso where she died,
the coroner examined
the failed liver and swollen brain. Then,
Jakelin's chest and head were stitched up
and she returned to Guatemala
in a short white coffin
to her mother, grandparents,
and dozens of women preparing
tamales and beans to feed the grieving.
In Q'eqchi', *w-e* means *mouth*.

· · ·

Alloy

An Apostrophe for Isamu Noguchi

Is stone the opposite of dust? And if so, are we then stone before dust?
    And before that, some kind of betwixt? The mush inside a
    translucent chrysalis turning cellophane-clear when, of a
    sudden,
you can see the monarch throbbing and scratching its way into air—

unlike a centipede that lays eggs, even curls around them with her
    hundred feet. You said that *living in Japan*
our house was filled with centipedes. I became rather fond of them; I lost my
    fear. You know, when you kill one, the two halves just walk off.
Surely they played in your mind all the way to your piece "Even the
    Centipede,"

molded from Ibaraki clay—though you felt *in a medium like clay*
    anything can be done;
and stated, *I think that's dangerous. It's too fluid. Too facile.*
Under your instruction, I'll find what's too fluid for me and turn my
    scratching away from facile to fossil

using hammer, chisel, and drill if lucky enough to come across the
    right quarry and ask nice enough or pay enough
for a crew to blast out the marble—unless the material is residue from
    something else. *Glacial pain?*
I mean, *glacial moraine*

from my home near the Sound where a glacier once aborted boulders
        onto these lean beaches.
I pick up a rock rounded and chipped in the surf, then, back home,
        like those who set Jizo on boulevard altars in Kyoto,
I tie a bib around its belly then place it on our mantel. Like those
        women, I, too, remember my baby unborn from betwixt and

Japanese. Japanese like those on the land where dust storms blew farm
        families to smithereens, then, blew desert
through rows of barracks surrounded by barbed wire and gunner
        watchtowers. Even orphan babies,
with one drop of *Jap blood*, were seized from whatever charity to live in
        bowls of dust. And you, Noguchi-sensei,

volunteered yourself into this incarceration limbo with the goal to
        build a baseball diamond, swimming pool, and cemetery;
you entered Poston Internment, where you knew yourself a Nisei, that
        is, without the rights of a citizen: *request*, of course, *denied*.
(Not for nothing, you were despised on both sides.) And as for
        centipedes

I'm not so much afraid as squeamish, which is different, and I've
        never killed one by cutting it in half
so I don't know about the two alive sides. The split selves not seeing
        eye-to-eye, I know only too well.

You knew and I know differently from parents who realized alloy only
    from without, whereas the *coywolf*, say,
realizes coyote and wolf even if the composite isn't brought to light—

maybe light is the opposite of stone, say, lightning that cracks inside a
    cloud? or coral that glows below the surface of the sea?
or the full moon that illuminates the shoji of the falling-asleep boy?
    I love the firefly's serenading signals, patterned according to
    kind. Kind—
something our parents did not essentially heed.

In my mind, stone, water, light, etcetera all come down to dust on a
    moth's wing that's evolved
to keep her patterns cued for a mate and to keep her blanketed in the
    stunning night.

In my mind, an alloy is ultimately practical *because*, as you commented,
    to be hybrid anticipates the future.

You also admitted: if you only have clay on hand, then from clay even
    the centipede is cast.

charms v.

Empathy

If you see a dragonfly caught
In a spider's barbed-wire
Endeavor to offer asylum
For compassion to fly ever higher

• • •

Divine

Song Yang wanted to work the recalcitrant farm,
to pick ginseng with her grandmother;
catch iridescent butterflies by the iridescent river. Five years later,
street-name Sisi, she worked in a realm
of under-the-table massage parlors,
a stone's throw from where I teach Intro. to Literature
to one hundred undergraduates,

Color — Caste — Denomination — / These — are Time's Affair —

Picking up Heineken, Red Bull and rotisserie chicken
from a bodega on Kissena, Sisi could realize
Death's large — Democratic fingers

But can I realize the line, merely having pored over Dickinson
where the Hudson River overwhelmed its banks—?

Sisi, forced to blow a dirty cop, gun held to her head,
thought of ginseng fields, the chit-chatting river, the factory
      dormitory

with her butterfly collection pinned to the curtain, while I
lectured to luminous undergraduates on
Death's diviner Classifying

•

—lectured that oblivion within a chrysalis
embodies the democratic; suggested
that there the Tenets are
                    put away and *put behind*;
recited lines to my immigrant students, my homeless students, my
working-graveyard-shift students who likely get
the more obvious instar

doing whatever they do outside our elegiac quadrangle. Certainly—

•

whether Astoria, Corona, Ozone Park—
my students living three generations under one roof
know better than I that only Death can
                    Rub away the Brand —

•

and yes, these students already know poetry, yes,
they recite Meng Haoran,
say, in the lexicon intimated in utero.

Chrysalis of Blonde — or Umber — / Equal Butterfly —

I murmur to a bleeding-heart.

                              •

Sisi's rivals deemed her dogged until
fleeing an undercover cop, she stepped to her sooty balcony,
over a mop and rail, to drop into neon air

back to Song Yang, to the line
                    As in sleep — all Hue forgotten —

then died in the careless ambulance.

Diviner also *divining* and so *virgula divina*, to locate,
intuit, foretell, foreshadow:

over the Flushing tarmac and concrete, over
the Unisphere and Kosciuszko,
my Grandmother Ghost and Mother Spirit

mingle into the egalitarian air and hover above
me in my lecture hall where I belong

speaking of and to foreign bodies

— Branded and Ablaze —

The Nest in Winter

In the father's shadowy hoard
pillows belch feathers across
mattress and floors:
what was an oriental rug, now
a carpet of scat, gone-astray socks,
calendars from rescue shelters
angling for checks.
There's nothing to toss
among the vivid tethers to
Mother. Maybe my mother, maybe Father's.
There's no margarine container
any less pathetic than
a netsuke from Kyoto;
no expired sardine tin less urgent
than a dozen aerograms; no
receipt less intimate
than their honeymoon photo
snapped in the local aquarium.
The adult daughter takes in
the spew,
pabulum that a bird feeds its nestling.

•   •   •

After Words for Ava

Off the Haiku beach,
that shoreline of sugarcane ash

where Grandma gave birth to Mama,
I snorkel and hear an iambic whoosh

I imagine as the sound of death but really

it's my breath while spying a triggerfish
     humuhumunukunukuapua'a

—later I will hear the sound again
this time the whooshing in utero

of the daughter of my daughter,

the most outlandish and earthly
foreign body
       whom we will call *Ava*—

    •   •   •

Nitro

More on Japanese Poetics

> *Downcast*
> *my body is a reed*
> *torn at the root—*
> *at a current's notice*
> *I'd acquiesce—I think*

—ONO NO KOMACHI (mid-ninth century)

I want arousal. I want to place the craft of poetry back where it belongs: that is, not *just* party to the mind, but a thing coursing throughout the body. Riotous and iambic. Other times, faint.

PLAYING

For *Brain Fever*, I wrote "Luminous Vapours," a short essay on word play. I wanted to speak about paronomasia, that fancy term for puns. Both English and Japanese traditions have influenced my sensibility not just for the jazziness of play, but more, because I love how multiple meanings can give way to a bit of unconscious material. In revision I like to pressure a word to detonate its denotations: *alarm*, both *an anxious awareness of danger* and *a kind of clock*; also, *alarm* is a noun and a verb. So, to place the image of an alarm clock by the bed is to suggest an emotional alarm. Words can be as unstable as nitroglycerin.

Such changeability can make for productive ambiguity: a simple word becomes a portal out of its dictionary definitions *and* out of logical sense. Such usage resists easy context and linear thinking. In everyday life, one can pick up on a suggestive remark, as when Mae West says, "I used to be Snow White . . . but I drifted." English literature has its most famous punster in Shakespeare's Hamlet. Literary allusion, of course, expands meaning. And T. S. Eliot's character Prufrock is full of such references when he admits, "I am not Prince Hamlet, nor was meant to be . . ."; and when he asks, "Would it have been worth while, / . . . To have squeezed the universe into a ball" (an ironic nod to Andrew Marvell's "To His Coy Mistress"). Any of these literary moments can suddenly blur one's vision, then create a leap from point A to points B, C, D. A wayward clarity.

Ambiguity is even more crucial in Japanese poetics. In a haiku, one word can explode the seventeen-syllable economy. Reading the word *iro,* one moves from the literal meaning *color* to *sexual desire;* reading *matsu,* from *pine tree* to *waiting.* In my poem "Constant Objection," I have the word "object" convey the verb *mind* and *resist,* as well as the nouns *body, stuff, organism, meaning, purpose, idea, hope, butt, doodad;* and in other poems, I use the idioms *object lesson, foreign object, constant objection, direct object, object theory.* Also in "Constant Objection," I hope that the phrase "yawning strippers" presents both bored girls as well as the vagina dentata, an image that would be a terrifying and indelible moment for the little boy viewer. In "Object Lessons," the closure depends on understanding that the noun *stay* (i.e., a literal plastic collar stay) includes the verb *to stay,* the sense of a child's plea, *Mother, stay.* And from "A Dusting," the *vacuum* in the line "The mother lived in a vacuum" must convey the literal vacuum cleaner *and* a space devoid of matter.

More associative and less pun-like, I hope that the opening line in "Foreign Body"—"This is a poem on my other's body, / I mean, *my mother's body*"—presents a Freudian slip where the speaker means to say *mother* but, in inadvertently saying *other,* reveals something compromising. (Had I been a diligent scholar in graduate school, I'd be able to cite William Empson's *Seven Types of Ambiguity.*) After all, aren't word associations the raw material of the psyche, where one rubs up against one's dreams?

PIVOTING

Ambiguity is rife in the "vocabulary-poor" Japanese language, where there is a wealth of homonyms. At least three poetic conventions depend on such word play. I am most interested in *kakekotoba* or "pivot-word": "a scheme of word play in which a series of sounds is used to mean two things at once by different parsings" (Miner, 162). The word "parsing" strikes me as useful for analytical readings, but not necessarily for a reader who is experiencing the poem as opposed to mentally examining it during a first read. *Experiencing is a physical event.* As such, I think of a pivot-word as the site of an opening, of potential explosion. Further, the moment is more pointed than the shift found in a sonnet's volta; and the placement of the pivot-word is crucial (and not predetermined). In the following line-by-line transliterations, I have used capitalization to indicate the pivot-word in each of the following poems by Ono no Komachi.

hito ni awamu	he will not come
TSUKI no naki yo wa	moon/chance
omoiokite	I think and
mune hashiri hi ni	*inside my pounding chest*
kokoro yakeori	heart is seared

Hiroaki Sato writes in a footnote to his translation: "*Tsuki*, given here as 'moon,' also has the sense of 'means,' so the opening part of this poem also says: 'On this night I have no means of meeting him'" (Sato, *Japanese Women Poets*, 49). The pivot comes early and casts a sense of darkness and dejection on the rest of the poem. It is interesting to note how famous translators have rendered the moon/chance pivot:

<u>On such</u> a night as this
When no <u>moon</u> lights your way to me   Earl Miner

This night of no <u>moon</u>
<u>There is no way</u> to meet him.   Donald Keene

<u>No way</u> to see him
on this <u>moon</u>less night—   Jane Hirshfield with Mariko Aratani

This <u>moon</u>less night I <u>can't</u> meet him   Hiroaki Sato

The English versions are not as economical and therefore not as intense. There is no pivot moment. In Hirshfield's choice of "see," she suggests both literally being able to see someone and the vernacular "seeing," as in a liaison. Sato implies that there is no chance by using the word "can't." Here is my attempt:

no chance of his visit
without the moonlight—
so thinking

within my pounding breast
my heart blazes—

I've added the two literal meanings for *tsuki*, but, sadly, I cannot achieve the compression that the Japanese engenders. Implication may be a satisfying solution, but it does not express the intensity that the double meaning poses. Here is a second attempt:

he will not visit
without the moon casting a light—
so thinking
within my pounding breast
my heart blazes—

I am trying to find words related to the image of the moon that have the same suggestive power. The word "cast" means *throwing [off]*, *directing [eyes]*, *causing [light] to appear, discard,* the phrase *cast a spell*; the idioms *cast doubt, cast lots, cast adrift.* It is not a poor solution, but finally pales, so to speak.

Here is a second Ono no Komachi poem:

IRO miede	color [complexion; *also refers to* sexual flush] seeing
utsurou mono wa	a thing that fades
yo no naka no	middle of the world's
hito no kokoro no	man's heart [and mind]'s
hana ni zo arikeru	flower is in it !

Brower and Miner (204) paraphrase the poem: *A thing which fades without its color visible is the flower of the heart of a man of the middle of the world (i.e., of this world).*

Here is my attempt at translation:

that flush—
what changes
in this world of

a man's heart and
its flower—

What are my reasonings behind this translation exercise? Another way to think of the pivot-word is, in my mind, a *portal* word. Because the poem erupts at that moment, the reader can *enter at the site for other possibilities.* Because Komachi started with *iro*, the poem keeps shifting its tonal color: *hana/flower, hito/man,* and *kokoro/heart-mind.* The progression in these thirty-one syllables radiates outward (Brower and Miner, 205). I hope that in my modest translation, *flush* can carry the ambiguity of *the facial glow from illness or embarrassment, a cleansing,* and even *driving a bird from its cover.* Finally, in both of my translation exercises, I have experienced again how to go with words that are marvelously "unstable."

JUXTAPOSING

Before commenting on how juxtaposition affects progression, I need to cite the translator Hiroaki Sato on the tanka form and its syllabic units (visible when lineated): as a "sense-making unit [the tanka became] a two-part poem of upper and lower hemistiches with a single strong caesura after 5-7-5" (Sato, *String of Beads*, 26–27). In such a way the Komachi poem would have been rendered vertically as one line. Here is the horizontal romanization:

iro miede utsurou mono wa yo no naka no hito no kokoro no hana ni zo arikeru

understood as:

IRO miede	color [complexion; *also refers to* sexual flush] seeing
utsurou mono wa	a thing that fades
yo no naka no	middle of the world's
[pause]	[pause]
hito no kokoro no	man's heart [and mind]'s
hana ni zo arikeru	flower is in it !

I have repeated the earlier transliteration for the sake of noting the progression and its "pause." In the upper section, color is central; in the lower, Komachi presents stark imagery that becomes the speaker's comparison and realization. The effect is a motion from the quiet, albeit passionate, real world to man's heart and the flower therein *plus* the exclamatory *zo* (translated as an exclamation point). I experience this sharp juxtaposition as a rhetorical whiplash that is absolutely physical.

Of course, Western poetics counts juxtaposition in its treasury of poetic terms: *parataxis*, or "two starkly dissimilar objects of ideas being place beside each other" (Hogue). Wallace Stevens comes to mind: " . . . her horny [dead] feet protrude . . . / The only emperor is the emperor of ice-cream." The excitement, in fact an epiphany, is in the odd side-by-side images of a corpse and ice cream. Yes, that sharp cut to comparison is absolutely experiential.

My challenge was to adopt this severe movement. I had assigned myself a kind of jump-cut exercise that produced "Charming Lines" (*The Artist's Daughter*). In part because I knew that my editor Jill Bialosky liked this piece, I thought to try more. "The Ashes" was scribbled. Here is the opening stanza:

The puppy snarfles to be let out
and I wake to radiator gurgling
then feet crunching the reticent snow.
Before I was born, Mother sewed her own suits.
What do her ashes know?

My wish is for the reader to shift from a moment of waking consciousness to a random realization and then to a question about human remains. My wish is for the reader to experience the odd shifts to awareness. My hope is that the experience is moving.

But if here or in other sections such juxtapositions just don't work, I will have failed this undertaking. Over the decades, I may have relied a bit too much on recklessness as a strategy to yield unconscious material and, by end, to offer a mental and emotional closure. To offer a *kabuki* trapdoor— but that is another story.

Finally, perhaps I should just let those who do not know anything about Japanese poetics just read without distraction. Perhaps I shouldn't feel the need to essay my mixed sensibility. Please, dear reader, please count this not as a lecture, but as an abiding homage to a culture that is both foreign and embodied.

Essay Influences and Sources

Brower, Robert H., and Earl Miner. *Japanese Court Poetry*. London: The Cresset Press, 1962.

Hahn, Tomie. *Sensational Knowledge: Embodying Culture through Japanese Dance*. Middletown, CT: Wesleyan University Press, 2007.

Hogue, Chelsea. "Parataxis." *LitCharts*. LitCharts LLC, 5 May 2017.

Miner, Earl. *An Introduction to Japanese Court Poetry*. Stanford, CA: Stanford University Press, 1968.

Sato, Hiroaki. *Japanese Women Poets: An Anthology*. Armonk, NY: M. E. Sharpe, 2008.

Sato, Hiroaki. *String of Beads: Complete Poems of Princess Shikishi*. Honolulu: University of Hawaii Press, 1993.

Afterword

The Bamboo Grove Where Various Individuals Mostly Think Aloud

> The light grew fainter until the cedars and bamboo were lost from sight.
>
> RYŪNOSUKE AKUTAGAWA, "In a Grove"

The Daughter

I told the appraiser, what charmed our parents is now what makes the house *unsalable*: fifty stone steps leading up to a house secluded in trees and treetops. No one would ever visit, except the meter man and the occasional Jehovah's Witness—who our father always chased off.

The Granddaughter

At Grandpa's funeral, Mom and Auntie both spoke of their childhood memories, both so different. Had I been offered the chance, I wondered what I would've said. On the train home, I jotted down:

Mothballs.

Lacquering a bamboo bracelet. Carving a linoleum block, then printing the picture (mine, a turtle).

The fifty-two slippery stone steps that Mom had to sweep or shovel when she was a teenager.

Learning to use chopsticks with a rubber band and wad of paper making something like tweezers.

Seven years after Grandma died, Grandpa took us to Hong Kong where we rode a tram up The Peak and I ate bad hamburger and he wouldn't let me call Mom "because it's long distance." That must have been when Mom and Dad were separating and we didn't know because they didn't ever argue.

In the garden patch behind their house, digging in the compost for worms to feed
   Turt, the turtle.
A doll whose heart lit up in the dark. Waffle iron.
In restrooms Grandma would cover the toilet seat with paper for me.
Learning to sift flour.

I am not sure if I remember the smell of mothballs from staying at the house or, if after Grandma died, just from Grandpa's clothes. I think in the ten years after she died, I only went back to the house a few times. I didn't want to sleep in that bedroom where I'd slept with Grandma under a comforter, even in summer. Grandpa *was* that mothball smell.

The Appraiser to the Two Daughters

Honestly, there's no low-balling here. I mean, the stone steps—who'd want to climb them? No garage. No car access (even for a dumpster). Septic tank, yes? Well water? I mean I can't believe there's so much rock.

The Appraiser again to the Daughters

The cost to demolish may be greater than the property value. No offense, but the house is worth nothing.

The Daughter again

After Mother died, Father's various art projects took on their real shapes: stacks of egg crates and envelopes of beer labels. Buckets of water with soaking bamboo.

The Daughter again

Then of course, a jumble of junk mail so dense you couldn't see the floor. Flowerpots with no plants, with only soil.

The Father

It. Is. My. House. Why are those girls telling me I can't go to my house. I'm going to hail a taxi and take it the whole damn twenty-five miles. *Balls.*

The Father to the Daughters

I had planned, we always did, to dig up bamboo shoots, then parboil them for the girls. But when the bamboo took over the property—even threatening to invade the neighboring yard, even threatening, I think, the foundation of the house—I hired guys to come over and rip it out by the roots. Then they returned and stole a samurai dagger and an antique silk jacket.

Father's Second Wife to the Daughters

You know, all these ten years—or is it nine—anyway, all these years I have never been in that man's home. He would stay with me most of the week, then return to his house *to water the bamboo*, etc. etc. At one point I told him that if he didn't invite me inside, we could just break up. Well that deadline came and went.

The Daughter again

She just didn't get it: how a fastidious dresser, a man who picked lint off the Oriental, might have a home in absolute ruin. She tried mightily to contain the projects that he produced in her apartment and she did pretty well. Even so, when she died I had to haul out everything from sketchbooks to scraps of bamboo. Lots of pieces.

The Second Daughter to Sister

I don't know when his forgetfulness became a thief—ha! I mean *belief*—that there were guys breaking in.

The Deceased Wife to her Husband

You weeded and watered the garden of moss. The moss we'd found and replanted and never thrived, not really. But the bit of bamboo you planted certainly did. So much so that, when you stopped driving and stopped going up to the house, those several plants took over the whole half-acre lot. Along with stinging nettles.

The Second Daughter again

I've searched online for the tiny burrs that fasten to our pants when at the house. Even back at home, taking darks out of the dryer, I find the sharp things still fastened, even transferred to other clothing. And I am still not sure what the little devils are called.

The Second Granddaughter

Rei should add: *The bamboo cricket cage. And the paintings of the bamboo cricket cage.*

The Appraiser again to the Daughters

Let me know what you decide.

. . .

Notes

Epigraph
The lines are an excerpt from Charles Wright's poem, "College Days."

"*Object Lessons*"
I have used quotations and information about Dr. Chevalier Quixote Jackson gleaned from a number of sources, most notably from Mary Cappello's remarkable book *Swallow: Foreign Bodies, Their Ingestion, Inspiration, and the Curious Doctor Who Extracted Them* (New York: The New Press, 2011). Most of the italicized sections are from her book; a few italicized words are for emphasis.

"*Hatchlings*"
This poem was cut from *Toxic Flora* (2009), then revived last year. I believe the original source was "Calls from Crocodile Eggs Serve as Alerts" by Henry Fountain, *The New York Times*, June 24, 2008.

"*The Cryptic Chamber*"
The erasure material was taken from "Loving the Chambered Nautilus to Death" by William J. Broad, *The New York Times*, Science section, October 24, 2011.

"Cryptic" is a found piece from "Nautilus," *Wikipedia*, 2012.

"*She Sells Seashells*"
I have benefited from Shelley Emling, *The Fossil Hunter* (NY: Palgrave/MacMillan, 2009) and Thomas W. Goodhue, *Curious Bones: Mary Anning and the birth of paleontology*. (Greensboro, NC: Morgan Reynolds Publishing, Inc., 2002).

The following lines are from Lord Byron:

> *'Tis time this heart should be unmoved,*
> *Since others it hath ceased to move . . .*

Black Ven is a cliff in Dorset, England, that is part of what is known as the Jurassic Coast.

"Likeness—A Self-Portrait"

Quoted material is from the article "Blink Twice if You Like Me" by Carl Zimmer, *The New York Times*, June 29, 2009. I have taken some poetic license with the information.

"After Being Asked If I Write the Occasional Poem*"*

I used material from "In Home Village of Girl Who Died in U.S. Custody, Poverty Drives Migration" by Elisabeth Malkin, *The New York Times*, December 18, 2018.

"Alloy"

I have used quotations and information about Isamu Noguchi gleaned from a number of sources, including *Isamu Noguchi: Essays and Conversations*, edited by Diane Apotolos-Cappadonna and Bruce Altshuler (New York: Harry Abrams Publishers, 1994); and Masayo Duus, *The Life of Isamu Noguchi: Journey without Borders*, translated from the Japanese by Peter Duus (Princeton, NJ: Princeton University Press, 2004).

"Divine"

I have used some details from "The Case of Jane Doe Ponytail," by Dan Barry and Jeffrey E. Singer, *The New York Times*, October 16, 2018. In a follow-up article published after this poem was written ("'Jane Doe Ponytail': Her Life Ended in N.Y. Now Her Brother's Bringing Her [Ashes] Home," *NYT*, April 9, 2019), the same journalists reported that Song Yang's mother and brother did not believe the official account of her death and conducted their own investigation.

The italicized phrases and lines are from Emily Dickinson's "Color — Caste — Denomination — " [836]. The Unisphere was built for the 1964 N.Y. World's Fair, and the Kosciuszko is a bridge connecting Brooklyn and Queens.

"After Words for Ava"
The *humuhumunukunukuapuaʻa* is Hawaiʻi's state fish.

"Afterword: The Bamboo Grove Where Various Individuals Mostly Think Aloud"
I've adopted Rashōmon points of view, as made famous by the film based on Ryūnosuke Akutagawa's combined short stories, "Rashōmon," and "In a Grove."

Acknowledgments

My tremendous thanks to the writers who took time from their own art to read and comment on these poems: in particular to Nicole Cooley, Lynn Emanuel, Paul Lisicky, Stephen Miller, Rajiv Mohabir, Dara Weir, Abby Wender, and my dear husband Harold Schechter. Thanks also to Beowulf Sheehan for his magic lens. And my gratitude to the editors who took the poems listed below. And, as always, abiding thanks to Jill Bialosky for her confidence and friendship.

American Poetry Review
    "*She Sells Seashells*"

Believer
    "A Little Safe"

Bosch Bruegel Anthology
    "Unearthly Delights"
This poem was written for a planned ekphrastic anthology edited by David Sullivan, and I thank him for the "assignment." I dearly hope the collection will be realized.

Boston Review online
    "A Dusting"

Epiphany Editions Chapbook
    "The Cryptic Chamber"

Hanging Loose
    "Afterword: The Bamboo Grove Where Various Individuals Mostly Think Aloud" (published as "The Bamboo Grove")

jubilat
    "Object Lessons"
    "The Old House Speaks"
    "Constant Objection"

Kenyon Review
        "Likeness—A Self-Portrait" (published as "Brilliance: A Valentine")

Los Angeles Review of Books
        "Three Charms from *Foreign Bodies*"

Ploughshares
        "Alloy—An Apostrophe for Isamu Noguchi"

Plume
        "Hatchlings"
        "Divine" (published as "The Diviner")

Poetry
        "The Ashes"
        "Foreign Body"

The New Yorker
        "After Being Asked if I Write the *Occasional Poem*"

Quarternote Chapbook series, Sarabande Books
        "Sparkly Things" (published as "Father's Nest")

The Kiss anthology (WWN, 2018)
        "Another Poem for Maude" (published as "For Maude")

The Yale Review
        "The Nest in Winter"

Dedication

When asked, "What does it look like to be an artist?" I said, "My father came home after teaching middle school, ate an early dinner, turned on the tv in the living room, set up his card table, and painted."

in memory of my father